Holy Flavours

Vol-1 - Eat the Rainbow Raw Meals

Nidhi Jagetia

ISBN 13: 978-93-90976-33-1
ISBN 10: 93-90976-33-2

Printed in India and published by BUUKS.

References: shutterstock.com, freepik.com, pixabay.com

Contents

Acknowledgement

With my full heart and deepest gratitude, I would like to thank everyone who has come into my life and inspired me in some way through their presence. Writing a book is a lengthy process. I would like to specially thank my dad to push me into writing a book and whose love and support knows no limit. I would also like to thank my mom for her huge support and contribution in creation of so many holy flavours, it would not be possible without her. I would like to thank my brother Nikunj for motivating and supporting me. I am thankful to my cousin Shruti and all my amazing extended family. Shreya, Akansha & Abhijeet and all my friends for generously sharing their love and being a constant support. It would not be possible without you all.

To the awesome human beings that make up my team- Photographer- Himalaya, my left-hand Monika, my house help and the entire team of Buuks especially Roshni for giving life to my imagination. Very thankful and grateful to have found these supporters.

Nidhi Jagetia

Welcome

Welcoming you to a fresh start, I am very thankful and happy that you are starting this journey of healthy living. You will fall in love with food in a different way. We do not eat food just for the taste, it is a form of energy, it is an emotion.

I am incredibly grateful that I started making this kind of a connection with food after eating consciously and creating lively recipes. All the lovely combinations and golden thoughts are jotted in this book.

The beauty of nature & available seasonal resources is the abundance of flavour in the fruits and vegetables. At Holy Flavours, we use all these natural flavours to make the best combinations to savour the taste buds as well as nourish the body.

All the best on this journey of yumminess. Let's get you started on a new relationship with food.

Enjoy making these delicious recipes. Connect with me on social media. I would love to see your pictures and hear about your own inspired recipe creations.

What is your relationship status with food?
☑ I eat to live.
☐ I live to eat.

Nidhi Jagetia

About the Author

Hey,

I am Nidhi. I am a daughter, sister, friend, nature lover & a health consultant.

My purpose in life is to help people understand the beauty of living in alignment with nature by working with natural foods and change in lifestyle habits to regain true health.

My journey started when I was young, full of energy and started studying the science of natural living and healing from Mumbai & later Australia. It felt rewarding to see people around me healing from Diabetes, Thyroid, Obesity & other lifestyle disorders by using the only key of right natural nutrition, whole plant-based foods & happy living.

This book has the basic yet flavourful creations to satisfy your taste buds & making raw eating simple

Holy Flavours will help you to take the leap and make the right choices for your plate. This also means the recipes will make plants taste YUM & nourishing! But more than that, it will help build a new connection with food. You can call this conscious eating.

You are not so far to gain immense positive returns by eating just the right foods.

Fall in love with all the amazing combination and let me know how you go!

Lots of Love,
Nidhi Jagetia

   ▶ - healandbeyond

Everything About Raw Nutrition

SCAN ME

What is *Nutrition*?

Nut is a prefix that comes from the latin word – 'Nux' which means beginning point, seed or point of light. Nutrition is the process of getting 'life' or 'light' into one's body; literally to 'nurse' or to suckle upon light.

There are 7 known ways of taking in the sunlight, and eating plants is one of them. Plants synthesize light from the sun and other elements to sustain themselves.

When we chew the plant in our mouths it is called making bolus. This process is how whole foods become recognizable by the cells of our body as sunlight or photo-electro chemical messages. Our body's cell only understands this language of sunlight. Hence by feeding raw we are supporting our own life by feeding on the sunlight.

Raw food is not uncooked it is sun-cooked food.

This is exactly how our ancestors described 'raw'. Infact 'raw' is name of the SUN god in Ancient Egypt. Hence by the term 'raw meals' it means a real plant growing in soil, air, sunshine & water. It is full of life and vitality. The moment we eat that raw lively plant, it hydrates & nourishes each part of our body. A raw meal has all the enzymes, juices & essential oils needed for our system to carry the 60,000 activities happening every second inside the body. It literally empowers our whole system.

When a seedling grows and become a plant, it is literally an edible form of sunshine. The fruit grown on the tree is nothing, but golden sunshine packed to feed and nourish the human body in the truest sense. Nothing can be as whole as that wholefood.

Let us observe and understand.

We are natural beings. Eating raw meals has always been a part of all our traditions. The comfort of cooked meals has replaced all the freshness of our meals and life. By eating sun cooked food, we get the maximum number of multivitamins, minerals & nutrition.

Let us also observe – Have you ever seen an animal overcooking or even cooking for that matter?

All living creatures on the planet, except for humans, eat their food in a raw form. No one has to tell the cow to eat grass or the bear to eat berries— they just do it. As humans have evolved, however, most people have been led away from nature and raw food.

Elephant is one the strongest mammal and all its strength comes from eating heaps of grass. They do not need protein supplements to make protein instead their body makes it with green grass, herbs, plants, fruits & sunshine available in the wild.

How logical does it seem? - It is always better to have a plateful of fresh seasonal mangoes than a slice of cheesecake. It is better to eat more chlorophyll rich greens, water rich fruits and healing vegetables than heavy oily, highly processed foods.

When an overcooked over-processed dead meal is eaten it has no life, hence it does not add much nutritional value. Uncooked plant foods are rich in enzymes, which are needed for the digestive system to work properly. Natural enzymes in fresh fruits and vegetables easily breaks down and the body processes them quickly and on the other hand excessive cooked food, passes through the digestive tract more slowly, allowing for fermentation and toxins to remain in the body. Toxins in the body can cause many problems, including hormonal turmoil, fatigue, arthritis, intestinal discomfort, skin eruptions, headaches, and much more.

The whole human generation is now more focused on cooking, overcooking, baking etc but the real essence, flavour & a plethora of nutritional benefits lie in the raw live plant. When you learn to make a satisfying raw food meal, many mysteries of raw food preparation unravel, and it becomes quite easy to include raw meals every day in your diet.

I am not outrightly rejecting the traditional cooked delicacies here; I am only highlighting how the human generation has distanced itself from fresh and plant-based foods and has only focused on consuming cooked meals in their day-to-day life. Changing the way, you eat will effectively change the way you feel, look and think. It happened with me and thousands of others who have incorporated a plant-based diet into their lives. It can happen to you once you decide to embrace a healthy eating lifestyle and a desire to feel energized and joyful. I feel eating healthy is the best way to show yourself some love.

The always asked question-

"How do you get your protein?"

Proteins, minerals, and vitamins can be obtained from a carefully crafted diet of dark leafy greens, nuts, seeds, fruits, and sprouts. Based on 700 studies, including Dr. Colin Campbell's "The China Study", we need only 5-6 % of total calorie intake to replace the protein regularly excreted by the body. Multiple studies show that eating natural vegan protein is much healthier for us than animal protein. If you consume a green drink daily or a large salad containing greens, you will easily fulfill your protein needs.

Spinach contains 49% protein; broccoli, 45%; lettuce, 34%; kale, 45%; Chinese cabbage, 34%; and sprouts like mung beans, 43%. Greens are higher in protein than fruits or nuts, but both are good sources of protein along with hemp seeds. The best part is that, they come with a bonus of vitamin, minerals, anticancer properties also.

Eating Raw Plant based foods is not just for your own health benefit but also for planet's better future, less violence & more love.

The 3 W's of eating Fresh Raw meals.

Raw food creates major health improvements. It completely fulfills the body's requirement of multivitamins, micronutrients & other essential minerals.

You will feel and look younger, be happier, and appreciate life better.

When you eat raw and fresh, the highly processed foods get out of your lifestyle. Processed foods have no nutritional value at all! They are loaded with fats, sugars, sodium, preservatives, and chemicals. Nearly every food found in a can, box or a pouch contains some type of preservatives with a high salt content.

When

Following the circadian rhythm of the sun to eat all the meals is the best way to utilise the natural juices of the organs to enhance the entire process of ingestion, digestion, absorption, assimilation & egestion.

Timing of meals is followed as per the timings of nature's clock.

Breaking the fast - 10:00 am
Wholesome Lunch - 1:00 pm
Healing Dinner - 7:00 pm

FIVE PROCESSES IN DIGESTION

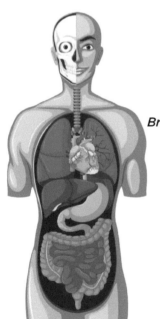

INGESTION
Taking in food.

DIGESTION
Breakdown of complex food substances into smaller soluble food substances.

ABSORPTION
Digested food is absorbed into body cells.

ASSIMILATION
Absorbed food is used to provide energy or form new protoplasm.

EGESTION
Removal of undigested food.

Who

The raw food meals eliminate many health issues, some of which are "age"-related symptoms.

If you are looking for food as an 'ultimate medicine' kind of lifestyle, this is the best way to boost your health routine.

Raw food is the basic human food and is very good for all age groups.

Stubborn weight is lost and not regained. Depression disappears. Soft and radiant skin within weeks. Need for over-the-counter drugs for headaches eliminate. Increases Energy. Improves Digestion. Brings clarity in thoughts and improves focus. One becomes better in tune with the body's needs. Risk of diseases, including diabetes, heart disease, cancer, arthritis, high blood pressure, and cholesterol, is reduced.

Adapting to raw fresh meals in the diet will help heal and nourish the body, mind & soul.

Spiritual Connection & Emotions

Why the Food You Eat is so Important for Spiritual Connection?

It's no secret that modern life can be stressful. There are so many things competing for our attention in this technological age that more and more of us are living in a constant state of stimulation. We are on the edge and forever 'wired.' For many of us, meditation or pursuing our passion is a beautiful way to find stillness and calmness of mind, but many people find this quite challenging. They can't get past their racing thoughts and fidgeting body.

What a lot of people don't realise is that the food you eat plays a vital role in your ability to reach that deep meditative and blissful state. If we fail to give our beloved nervous system the critical nutrients it needs to function optimally and remain calm, we can get stuck in the primal, reactive way of living which is unable to transcend into higher levels of awareness and making the body nutritionally stressed.

We eat without thinking about what our food is doing for our bodies and our connection.

'You are what you eat' is the old cliché that you are no doubt familiar with, but have you ever realised just how profound this notion is and applied it in your life?

We tend to eat out of our own as well as community habits. We eat without consciously thinking as to what this food is doing inside our body, beyond the momentary taste sensation in our mouth. To achieve tasteful combinations, many harmful practices are now introduced in food preparation. This is all because we have become so disconnected with the natural world and knowledge of where our food actually comes from.

We, as homo sapiens, have somehow come to a point in our lives where we no longer intuitively know what is correct for us to eat.

Let that sink in for a moment!

Why is it that we are the only species on Earth to have this problem?

There is not a single animal living in its natural environment that is overweight or suffering a chronic illness because of their diet. They just know what to eat. They are in touch with the innate intelligence that drives their food choices, and as a result, they thrive. If this alone doesn't show how spiritually disconnected, we have become, I don't know what will.

To keep the body in good health is a duty, for otherwise we shall not be able to light the lamp of wisdom and keep our mind strong and clear. – Buddha

Connecting with Food, Connecting with Source

How does this all link to our practice of eating raw foods?

The answer is simple. We are not eating real food anymore. The problem we now face is an overabundance of chemically laden products masquerading as foods, and a system that makes it difficult to acquire quality plant food, which is what we require the most. We are eating 'food like products' that our biology does not recognize, which results in a state of physiological stress. Eating raw form of plants is the best way to absorb the energy and nutrition for our best spiritual growth.

Food is Energy

Every fruit, vegetable & plant around us has energy levels. In fact, even pure water has an energy aura. When we are eating the plant raw, that energy is transmitted to our body and makes us more energetic and vibrant.

Not just this, the nature has food replicas that mirrors the human organs they nourish. This study is called Doctrine of Signatures.

Looking at some interesting comparisons:

A slice of carrot from a distance, can easily resemble an eye, and on closer view reveals a pattern of radiating lines that mimics the pupil and iris. Countless studies show it improves blood flow to our eyes and prevents macular degeneration.

A tomato when cut from the top looks like a heart with 4 chambers of the heart. The American Heart Foundation says it's the best food for your heart because of its lycopene content.

A walnut looks exactly like the brain. Baylor University has found omega 3-6-9's in walnuts that cross the blood brain barrier enhancing brain function and the fats are perfect for growth and repair.

Coincidence? Possibly.

When a wholefood is cooked, the energy aura of the food decreases changing the beneficial properties of the food. Excessive cooking, heating & frying completely changes the chemistry and electromagnetic energy of the original food. Hence the power that a food possesses, which is a blessing to humankind, is destroyed and it becomes more acidic and highly inappropriate to eat & digest further making the body toxic in later stages.

Food and Emotions

We now know the benefits and impact of fresh food upon our body.

Let's examine the more subtle processes that affect us and our body. The two most powerful tools one uses to create experiences in the physical world are the mind and emotions. Our physical body is just a clay shell that carries our awareness around. We would not be able to create the events in our life if it were not for the thought processes that allows us to imagine the sequence of events we wish to experience. Without the emotions, however, there would be no desire to create. As the mind takes images of the past and present and puts them together to create the future, it is the emotions that drive us to manifest these images.

All the toxicity in the mind and body happens due to imbalance in thoughts and foods. I believe a person first thinks and then achieves thoughtfulness of being a conscious eater not just for the world but for our own self. This will help reduce numerous visits to hospitals and save us from the cost and side-effects of medicines and harmful treatments.

The mind and emotions can either work for us in a positive manner by enhancing and revitalizing our health, or against us in a negative manner by controlling and enslaving us. Whatever a person creates mentally and emotionally becomes their experience. True health and vitality are achieved when our mental and emotional "bodies" are in balance. Each of these bodies impact one another.

Emotions, especially the negative ones like anger, hate, and jealousy, can make the physical body sick and full of diseases. These emotions are stored in the liver and kidneys. Emotions can even shut down our mind, affecting our ability to comprehend, think and make rational decisions. A lack of emotional stability can close off the heart centres which drastically reduces our ability to get healthy, even to the point where death is the inevitable result. Love, happiness, joy, health and mental balance keeps the heart open. Unhappiness, depression, despair, anger, jealousy, rage, envy and negative states keep the heart center closed.

We sometimes use food to suppress and express emotions. We celebrate holidays and special occasions with food and drink and many times go overboard, throwing common sense out the window. Food is sometimes used as an entertainment. We diet, starve, binge, and purge ourselves to look like models. Food is used in many ways to deal with life's ups and downs.

One should start enjoying life for what it is. Observe nature and surround yourself with flowers and plants, as they are very healing. Nature embraces with energies of love. If we can let go of the past, we can enjoy every moment for what it is. Let all hate, anger, and opinions go.

Break out of the old, conditioned states of thinking and feeling and become vibrant and healthy. Do it now! Know your food, ask for love & balance.
Staying healthy can be challenging but fun at the same time. It should not be a chore. It is about rebuilding the entire body!

When we truly learn to eat for health and not solely for filling our stomach, we will be able to celebrate and thoroughly enjoy the right conscious choices of food for their nutritional value.

There is no magic pill and there never will be. Right nutrition and mindset are the only ultimate solution.

Basic Guidelines to Prepare

Food Combinations

For the most part, food combination is intuitive; we do what feels best for our bodies. If we are following the rule of eating seasonal produce, the food combination automatically becomes correct. Some combinations may work wonderfully for a person and not as well for others.

Melons are best eaten alone. They get absorbed into the body in fifteen minutes if eaten as a mono meal. Fruits are divided into groups such as acid, subacid, and sweet fruits. Mixing same category of fruits together is fine.

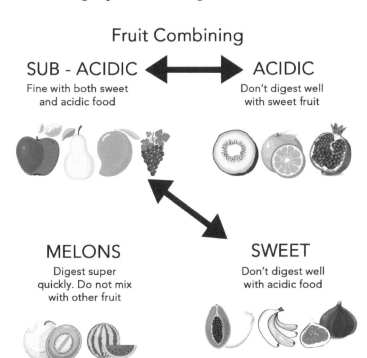

Fruit Combining

SUB - ACIDIC
Fine with both sweet and acidic food

ACIDIC
Don't digest well with sweet fruit

MELONS
Digest super quickly. Do not mix with other fruit

SWEET
Don't digest well with acidic food

The best sign as to whether we are properly combining food is to look at the quality of stool produced and the sensation that food gives to our body. When food is eaten in a proper combination, it makes us feel good and produce no flatulence, and the stool will be solid and will not contain any undigested food particles.

13

The Quality of Fruits and Vegetables

Eating Seasonal and Fresh
Throughout the year, most fruits transition from a fruiting stage to a dormant stage, to a leaf- and branch-growing stage, to a flowering stage, and then back again to fruiting. Each variety of fruit has its own cycle, some trees fruit in the summer, while others fruit in the spring or fall. Some trees fruit at different times based on their elevation or where, exactly, they are grown. To eliminate confusion, we should understand the cycles, contact a local farmer to learn what fruits & vegetables are in season according to where we live, and start keeping a local seasonal calendar.

The Organic Façade
Finding pure food has become a challenge in the modern world. Foods that are labelled "organic" can still be mass-produced, possibly using "natural" pesticides that are still toxic. (Purely natural pesticides such as bay leaves or marigolds are not harmful)
Even worse, brands may claim their food is organic when it is not. On the flip side, there are also pure, truly natural foods that are sold without the labels and high price tags which are usually associated with organic foods; it's just that the farmers who grow and sell them can't afford a certification as organic farmers.

To be sure that the produce is pure, grow it yourself or be conscious of where the food is coming from.

Hygiene and Storage

Washing
Do not wash fruits and vegetables with detergent or any kind of liquid. Instead use clean water to wash items. For produce with thick skin, use a vegetable brush to help wash away hard-to-remove microbes. Leafy greens with a lot of nooks and crannies like cauliflower, broccoli, strawberries, or lettuce should be soaked for 5 to 7 minutes in cold clean water.

Storing
It is better to store chopped fruits or salad in a glass or stainless steel. Do not consume very old, stored salad or fruits.

Raw Plant Based Milk

Nut Milk bags or muslin cloth is an amazing invention. Nut milk bags are useful little nylon bags used to separate nut milk from the pulp. They can be easily washed. Make sure they are dried well before you put them away in storage for next time. Be gentle, though — don't be too rough when squeezing out the nut milk as the bag could burst at the seams.

	Cashew Milk	Almond Milk	Coconut Milk	Sesame Milk	Other Nut Milk
Soak	5-6 hours	10 hours	Not required	10 hours	Avg 6-7 hours
Water : Nut	4:1 cup	4:1 cup	3:1 cup	3:1 cup	Depends
Sieve	Not required	Not required	Muslin cloth	Muslin cloth	If required
Storage	Refrigerate	Refrigerate	Refrigerate	Refrigerate	Refrigerate
Last	4-5 days	4-5 days	4-5 days	6-7 days	6-7 days

Soaking and Sprouting

Sprouts are amazing and easy to grow. They are an easy way to boost the nutrients intake. The vitamins content of the seed increases with sprouting. Sprouts also contain an enzyme to benefit the digestion process.

WEATHER

HUMID — Sprouting happens quickly, keep checking and shaking the sprouting seed's container during the process.

DRY — Sprouting happens moderately, splash water in between sprouting process to enhance the growth.

COLD — Sprouting happens slowly, keep at a warm place and sprinkle water if needed during the sprouting process.

HOT — Sprouting happens moderately, splash water in between sprouting process to enhance the growth and you can also refrigerate during the sprouting days if it is too hot.

STORAGE — Glass or steel container are the best to store.

SOAKING AND SPROUTING TABLE

	Soak time	Sprout time
Mustard	10 hours	3-4 days
Fenugreek	10 hours	3-5 days
Moong	8 hours	2 days
Alfa-alfa	10 hours	2-5 days
Sesame	8 hours	1-2 days
Millets	Hours vary depending on the millet	2-3 days

Raw Rainbow Meals Formula

Base Vegetable + Raw Dressing + Herbs to FLAVOUR + other flavouring vegetables.

1. Sprouts with a Twist

Sprouts are easy to grow and they are a power bundle full of benefits and nourishment.

INGREDIENTS-

- 2 Cups Freshly Grown Sprouts
- ¼ Cup Cucumber Finely Chopped
- ½ Cup Tomato Finely Chopped
- ½ Cup Onion Finely Chopped
- 4 Tbsp Pomegranate
- ½ Handful Peanuts
- 4 Tbsp Alfalfa Seed Sprouts, 2 Green Chilies, 1 Lemon, Salt and Pepper
- 1 Handful Finely Chopped Coriander Leaves

For Smoky Flavour-

- A Piece of Charcoal, 1 Tbsp Coconut Oil, Asafoetida.
- 1 Tbsp **#SELF-CARE**

METHOD-

For Dressings-
Simply mix the salt, lemon, black pepper, green chilies, peanut crunch.

For Salad-
Take a bowl with a lid, add fresh sprouts, cucumber finely chopped, tomato finely chopped, onion finely chopped, pomegranate. then add the dressing and mix well.

To make Smoky Flavour-
Step 1: Heat 1 charcoal piece such that it is fully red hot.
Step 2: Make a well in the centre of the bowl containing salad, place a small bowl in the well to put the hot charcoal. Place the hot coal inside the cup.
Step 3: Pour a spoon of coconut oil and a pinch of asafoetida on the hot coal. Now cover the bowl with the lid and make sure to not let the smoke escape the bowl. In 3-4 mins your salad will be completely flavoured.

2. Fermented Kimchi

The wealth of healthy bacteria and antioxidants in kimchi developed during the fermentation process exercise healing effects in the cardiovascular and digestive system. The flavonoids and probiotic rich kimchi help in strengthening the immune system and maintaining healthy levels of cholesterol.

INGREDIENTS-

For Kimchi-
– ½ Cup Purple Cabbage Kimchi (fermented for 4 - 5 days)
– ½ inch Grated Ginger
– 4-5 Minced Garlic
– 2-3 Green Chilies, Salt
– Handful Mustard Microgreens
– Lemon Juice
– 1 Tbsp Cayenne Pepper Powder
– ½ Tbsp Grated Lemon Zest
– 1 Tbsp #PATIENCE AND FAITH

For Salad-
– 1 Small Beetroot Grated or Spiralized
– 1 Carrot Grated
– ¼ Cup Pomegranate Seeds
– Shavings of Macadamia Nut (optional)

METHOD-

How to make Kimchi?
Step 1: Finely slice the cabbage into thin julienne (in shape of matchsticks) and remove the hard bits of the center. Soak the cabbage julienne in salt water for 2-3 hrs. Cover loosely with a clean tea towel. After 2 hours, rinse well under cold running water and drain well.
Step 2: Take a mixing bowl, and add the grated ginger, minced garlic cloves, cayenne pepper, green chilies, lemon juice, grated lemon zest and salt. Stir well until you have a paste.
Step 3: Now add the rinsed cabbage julienne back in and mix it thoroughly with the paste. Place the kimchi in a glass container at a warm corner of the kitchen to ferment for next 3-4 days.
Step 4: Check the kimchi every day, pressing the cabbage back under the surface. Start tasting after 3 days – it should be pleasantly sour – leave it for longer if necessary. It is subjective on the temperature and your personal taste. Once you are happy, you can place it in the fridge.

For Salad-
Take a bowl, add 3-4 tablespoons of fermented kimchi along with all the other salad ingredients. Garnish it with coriander leaves, mustard microgreens and macadamia nut shavings. Serve fresh.

*Tip - You will need to ferment the cabbage 2-3 days prior to make the kimchi salad. I used purple cabbage for this salad however you can use lettuce or green cabbage too.

3. Sweet Corn Bhel

This bhel is a perfect savoury meal for the day. The tasty drops of sauce on each corn makes the bhel very flavourful. Fresh small beads of raw sweetcorn are naturally sweet in taste and soft in texture and are full of fiber. It is extremely beneficial for your eyes, skin and hair.

INGREDIENTS-

For Bhel-
- 2 Cups of Raw Sweetcorn
- 1 Small Onion Finely Chopped
- 1 Small Red or Green Capsicum Finely Chopped
- A Small Sized Half Broccoli Floret Diced Evenly

For Dressing-
- 2 Green Chilies, Salt and Pepper
- 3 Tbsp Tamarind Dressing (Recipe 5 of Raw Dressings)
- 2 Tbsp Coriander Chutney
- 1 Tbsp #PASSION

METHOD-

For Dressings-
Mix the chopped coriander leaves, black pepper, finely chopped green chili with tamarind dressing and coriander chutney in a mixing bowl. Add a pinch of salt.

For Salad-
Add sweetcorn, onion, capsicum & broccoli floret ingredients into the bowl and serve fresh.

4. Tender Coconut Bowls

Coconut meat is found in the center of a young, green coconut. Coconut water helps nourish the fruit. As the coconut matures, some of the juice remains in liquid form while the rest ripens into the solid white flesh known as coconut meat. Coconut meat is beneficial for the kidney health and overall hydration of the body.

INGREDIENTS-

– 2 Coconuts Fresh Tender Coconut Meat (Malayi)
– 1 Cup Mashed Peas
– ½ Cup Thinly Sliced Spring Onion
– ½ Cup Finely Chopped Tomato
– ½ Cup Soaked Cashew
– 4 Tbsp Ginger Cashew Dressing
– ¼ Tbsp Cumin Powder, ¼ Tbsp Cayenne Pepper Powder, Coriander Leaves
– 1 Tbsp #FLEXIBILITY

METHOD-

For Ginger Cashew Dressing-
Mix soaked cashew, ¼ grated ginger and salt to make a smooth paste.

For Dressing-
Mix the cumin powder, cayenne pepper and coriander leaves.

For Salad Bowls-
Step 1: Place the coconut meat shaped in form of bowls on the chopping board.
Step 2: Place the mixture of mashed peas, thinly sliced spring onion and finely chopped tomato equally inside the coconut bowls.
Step 3: Serve it with the ginger cashew sauce & garnish with coriander.

5. Leafy Greens

Leafy green salad is full of chlorophyll and is superb for skin, blood circulation and hold numerous health benefits. Creamy and tangy flavour from peanuts and tomatoes makes this leafy green salad the most versatile option to eat.

INGREDIENTS-

If you do not have access to the below mentioned greens, please go for locally available leafy greens.

- 2 Cups Parallelly Cut Fresh Spinach
- ¼ Cup Parsley
- ½ Cup Lettuce
- Half Inch of Celery Finely Chopped
- ½ Inch Ginger
- 1 Garlic Clove
- 2 Cups Diced Tomatoes
- 1 Tbsp Peanut
- ½ Tbsp Coriander Seed, Salt, 2 Green Chilies, Pinch of Asafoetida
- 1 Tbsp #POSITIVE-MINDSET

METHOD-

For Dressings-
Combine tomatoes, green chilies, garlic, and salt in a mixer. Mix till you get a smooth paste.

For Salad-
Combine the parallelly cut raw spinach leaves and other greens in a mixing bowl along with the dressing prepared. Now garnish with hand grounded coriander seeds, peanut crunch & few pieces of tomato. Add salt as per taste.

Your chlorophyll rich leafy salad is ready to devour.

6. Cucumber Sev Puri

Cucumbers are amazing, crunchy and water rich. Making a sev puri from cucumber rings is one of my favourite raw meals. It is a burst of sweet and savoury flavours inside the mouth. A must try!

INGREDIENTS-

For Base-
– 1 Large Cucumber Sliced into Round Circles

For the First Layer of Topping -
– 1 Banana Mashed
– 2 Tomatoes Finely Chopped
– 2 Onions Finely Chopped
– Salt, Cayenne Pepper

For the Second Layer of Topping -
– 4 Tbsp Alfalfa Seed Sprouts
– ½ Cup Fresh Coconut Grated
– 4 Tbsp Classic Dates Dressing/ Chutney (Recipe 1 of Raw Dressings)
– 3 Tbsp Coriander Chutney
– 1 Tbsp #EXCITEMENT

METHOD-

For Topping-
Take a bowl & mix the mashed banana, tomatoes and onion. Add salt & cayenne pepper as per taste.

For the Sev Puri-
Step 1: Place the round cucumber slices in a plate.
Step 2: Add mashed banana topping mentioned above as the first layer.
Step 3: Splash a dash of both coriander and classic dates dressings on each slice.
Step 4: Top with grated coconut & alfalfa sprouts to garnish and make puffs for each bite.

7. Veggie Sticks Platter

Avocado is also called butter fruit. The creaminess of avocado with flavours of herbs makes this platter a flavourful tasty platter of goodness.

INGREDIENTS-

For the Dip-
– 1 Fully Ripe Avocado (you can also use mint leaves and soaked ½ cup cashews instead of avocado)
– 1 Small Red Onion Finely Chopped
– 1 Medium Tomato Finely Chopped
– 3-4 Cherry Tomatoes (optional)
– 1 Pinch of Asafoetida
– Salt, Pepper
– Lemon, Coriander Leaves, Green Chilies and Peanuts

For the Platter-
– 2 Carrot Sliced as Sticks, 1 Tomato Diced, 1 Cucumber Sliced as Sticks, 1 Medium Beetroot Thinly Sliced, 1/2 Radish Sliced as Stick, 12 Spinach Leaves Rolled in Pairs of Two.
– 1 Tbsp #WARMTH

METHOD-

For the Dip-
Mash avocado and simply mix onion, tomato with peanuts, lemon, salt, green chilies, coriander leaves and asafoetida to make a chunky creamy dressing.

For the Platter-
Serve the dip with sliced carrots, tomatoes, and spinach rolls.

24

8. Fresh Slaw

I love teaming raw pumpkin and coconut in a salad. The richness of coconut and dates enhances the taste of the whole salad. Pumpkin is one of the best weight loss foods and also helps the body fight viruses and infectious diseases.

INGREDIENTS-

For the Salad Grate-
– 1 Cup Grated Raw Pumpkin
– 1 Cup Shredded Raw Cabbage
– 1 Cup Grated Fresh Coconut
– ½ Sliced Spring Onion Greens
– 1 Finely Chopped Long Green Chili
– ¼ Tbsp Grated Turmeric Root (optional)
– 1 Tbsp **#NEW-BEGINNINGS**

For the Dressing-
– 4-5 Dates, 2 Garlic Cloves, 1 Green Chili, ½ Tbsp Apple Cider Vinegar, Salt, Pepper, Water

METHOD-

For the Dressing-
Mix all the ingredients in a mixer till it forms a beautiful brown paste.

For the Salad-
Combine the grated coconut, spring onions and grated pumpkin in a mixing bowl and add an enormous amount of dressing to hug every bite of the salad. Eat this combination immediately!

9. Zoodles

Zoodles are Zucchini noodles. Yes, you can use different spiralized veggies and make colourful dishes. Zoodle Salad looks very tempting and is also fun to eat. It is a hit with the kids as they love the spiral shape and different colours.

INGREDIENTS-

– 2 Zucchini Spiralized using a spiralizer
(If you do not have zucchini, you can use cucumber)
– 1 Full Sized Fully Ripe Tomato
– 2 Tbsp Avocado
– ¼ Cup Cashews Soaked for 3-4 hours
– ½ Tbsp Grated Ginger, 4-5 Garlic Cloves, 2 Long Green Chilies, 5-6 Basil Leaves
– Salt and Pepper
– 1 Tbsp #INNOVATION

Ingredients to Garnish-
– 4-5 Pieces Cauliflower Finely Chopped.
– 5-6 Cherry Tomatoes, 2 tsp Yellow Capsicum Finely Chopped

METHOD-

1. White sauce-
To make White Sauce Zoodles
Step 1: Make the white sauce in a high-speed blender by adding soaked cashews, basil, green chili, garlic, salt, and pepper. Blend it until it forms a smooth greenish-white paste.
Step 2: Mix the spiralized zoodles, chopped cauliflower, capsicum and white sauce.
Mix well with light hands so that the noodles don't break. Garnish well with oregano leaves, chili flakes. Eat the white zoodles immediately.

2. Red sauce-
To make the Red Sauce Zoodle
Step 1: Make the red sauce in a high-speed blender by adding 2 tbsp of avocado, 1 fully ripe tomato, ginger, garlic, chili and salt. Blend it until it forms a rich smooth paste.
Step 2: Mix the zoodles, chopped capsicum and red sauce. Mix well with light hands so that the noodles don't break. Garnish well with cherry tomatoes, oregano leaves and chili flakes. Eat the red zoodles immediately.

You can also mix both red sauce and white sauce to make pink sauce zoodles.

26

10. Mozzarella Bites

I got my creative juices flowing and after making some adjustments, I came up with this beauty. Each bite of the mozzarella is heavenly and cheesy. This salad tastes the best when the vegetables are fresh from your local farmer's market or vegetable stand. I hope you enjoy it!

INGREDIENTS-

For the Salad-
- 1 Cup Finely Chopped Carrot
- 1 Cup Finely Copped Spinach
- 1 Cup Microgreens
- ½ Cup Thinly Sliced Onion
- ½ Cup Small Beetroot Cubes
- Freshly Chopped Coriander
- 1 Tsp Oregano
- 1 Tsp Chilli Flakes
- Salt and Pepper.

For the Mozzarella-
- 100 gm Soaked Cashews
- 2 Tbsp Isabgol (Psyllium Husk)
- 2 Tbsp Lemon Juice
- 1 Tbsp #VIBRANT-THOUGHTS

METHOD-

For the Mozzarella-
Step 1: Soak Cashews in warm water for 2 hours.
Step 2: Add Isabgol in 400ml water and let it sit for 2 hours.
Step 3: Add soaked Cashews and Isabgol into the high-speed blender.
Step 4: Also add Lemon Juice + Rock salt as per taste+ 1 Clove of Garlic and fresh/dried herbs of your choice.
Step 5: Blend all ingredients to get smooth sliceable Mozzarella Cheese.
Step 6: Refrigerate for 1 day and use it with your salad.

For the Salad Platter-
Gently mix all the salad ingredients in a mixing bowl. Add the sliced mozzarella and the salad is ready to enjoy.

27

11. Raw Sushi

I have always loved the benefits of Nori, the seaweed superfood. It is an excellent source of iodine. The omega-3's in Nori helps create a natural oil barrier on the skin. This raw sushi is made with fresh vegetables rolled in a nori sheet.

INGREDIENTS-

For the Sushi Rice:
- 1 Cup Carrot Grated
- 1 Cup Cucumber Chopped
- ¼ Cup Celery Chopped
- ¼ Cup Fresh Coriander Finely Chopped
- ¼ Cup Finely
- ½ Teaspoon Ginger Grated
- 1 Tbsp #WELL-BEING

For the Sushi Rice Dressing:
- 3 Tbsp Sunflower Seeds (soaked for two hours)
- 5-6 Almonds (overnight soaked and peeled)
- Salt and Pepper

For the Mayo:
- 1 Cup Young Thai Coconut Flesh
- 3 Tbsp Raw Cashews (soaked overnight in water then rinsed and drained well)
- ½ Tbsp Freshly Grated Ginger
- 1 Small Chili
- 1 Garlic Clove
- 1 Tbsp Oregano
- ¼ Tsp Cayenne Pepper
- 1 Tbsp Lime Juice
- ¼ Tbsp Pepper
- A Pinch of Salt

–For the Sushi Ingredients:
- 2 Sheets of Nori
- 2 Long Strips Cucumber
- ½ Capsicum Cut into Strips.
- 4 Tbsp Alfalfa Sprouts
- Avocado Slices (as much as you like)
- Salt and Pepper

METHOD FOR SUSHI FILLING-

Mix the ingredients of Sushi Rice with Sushi Dressing in a Mayo Bowl

METHOD FOR ROLLING SUSHI-

Have all the salad filling ready. Lay the nori sheets on a flat work surface. Spread the "rice" evenly over 3/4th of each sheet. Arrange your salad filling on the "rice," add few drops of mayo, sprinkle with salt and pepper, then roll each sheet from an end that has been spread with "rice," finishing with the end of the nori that was left unfilled. Use a little water if necessary, to seal the seam. Cut and enjoy!

Raw Dressing Formula

Base Fruit/ Dry fruit/ Vegetable + Herbs + Spices + Sweet / Savoury FLAVOUR or both

1. Classic Dates

Classic Dates dip feels like the perfect sweet roadside chaat flavour. This juicy sauce gives a sweet twist to your palate

INGREDIENTS-

- 5 Pitted Dates
- 2 Cloves of Garlic
- 1 Tsp Organic Apple Cider Vinegar with Mother
- 1 Tsp Paprika Powder, ¼ inch of Ginger
- 1 Small Piece of Thai Chili, 1 Tbsp #SMILE

METHOD-

Firstly, blend dates and 20 ml of water. Add all the ingredients in the dates paste and blend till you get a smooth thick sauce.

Store in a jar and refrigerate. This can be used for 6-7 days.

2. Chili Raw Mango

The Chili Raw Mango is an appetising sauce which can be made during the season of raw mangoes. Raw Mangos are full of flavour and 1 Tbsp of this sauce can totally be a game changer for any salad.

INGREDIENTS-

- ½ Raw Mango
- 1 Pitted Medjool Dates
- 1 Greens of Spring Onion
- 1 Clove of Garlic
- 2 Long Red Chili
- 1Tbsp #FUN

METHOD-

Firstly, blend Mango and Medjool dates. Then add all the other ingredients and blend till you make a smooth paste. You can add water if needed.

Store the Mango Chilli Lime in a jar for 3 days tops. If you skip the spring onions the dip can be used for 6-7 days

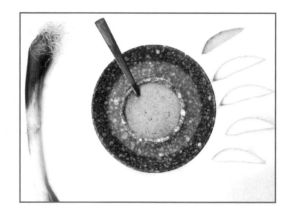

3. Mexican Sauce

Richness of tomatoes with a twist of smoked paprika gives this dip a rustic flavour. I love this sauce. It's a beautiful coloured perfect Mexican blend

INGREDIENTS-

- 1 Cup Sundried Tomato
- 5-6 Cherry Tomatoes or 1 Fully Ripe Tomato
- 1/4 Sweet Red Bell Pepper
- 1 Tbsp Jaggery Powder
- 2 Garlic Cloves
- ½ Tbsp Apple Cider Vinegar
- ¼ Tbsp Ground Cumin
- ½ Tbsp Dried Oregano
- ½ Tbsp Smoked Paprika Powder or Chili Powder
- A Pinch of Black Pepper
- 1Tbsp **#CHEERUP**

METHOD-

Blend all the ingredients with water to your desired consistency.

Store in a mason glass jar. This sauce lasts upto 7-8 days in the fridge.

4. Yellow Capsicum Wonder

Creating this creamy dressing is super easy. It has greatness of capsicum and thickness of cashew cream poured into one bowl.

INGREDIENTS-

- ¼ Cup-Soaked Cashews
- ½ Diced Yellow Capsicum
- 1 Tbsp Tahini (Recipe 8 of Raw dressing)
- 10-12 Leaves Basil
- 1/2 Green Chilies
- 2 Tbsp Lemon Juice OR Organic Apple Cider Vinegar with Mother
- Salt as per Taste
- 1Tbsp **#AMAZING LIFE**

METHOD-

Combine all the ingredients in a mixer jar and make a creamy smooth paste.

31

5. Tamarind Sauce

The tamarind sauce is a must have summer sauce which makes your tongue swirl and 1 Tbsp of this sauce can add a whole range of flavour to the veggies.

INGREDIENTS-

- 5 Pieces- Seedless Soaked Tamarind
- 2 Red Chilies
- 2 Tbsp Jaggery Powder
- A Pinch Black Salt
- 1/4 Tbsp Salt
- 1 Tbsp **#HAPPY DANCE**

METHOD-

Firstly, make the soaked tamarind paste, use a strainer to remove the non-chewable parts of tamarind.

Combine all the other ingredients in the tamarind paste & blend till you make a smooth runny tamarind dip. You can add water as per your requirement.

Store in a glass bottle. You can put the dip in deep freezer so that the taste is maintained.

6. Oregano Orange

A sweet citrusy combination to freshen the taste buds.

INGREDIENTS-

- 1 Orange Juice
- 1 Pitted Dates
- ¼ Sweet Red Bell Pepper
- 2 Tbsp Sunflower Seeds
- 2 Tbsp Dried Oregano
- ¼ Tbsp Organic Chili Powder
- A Pinch of Black Pepper Powder
- 1/2 Lemon Juice
- 1Tbsp **#SENSATION**

METHOD-

Blend all the above ingredients together with water to your desired consistency.

Store in a jar and refrigerate. You can use the oregano orange for 4-5 days.

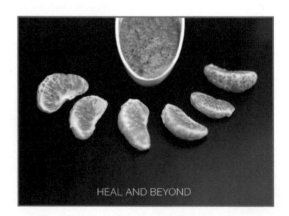

HEAL AND BEYOND

7. Guacamole Dip

I have tried hundreds of combinations of guacamole but this one right here is my favourite. The loud flavour of asafoetida combined with lemon is the key to make a lip-smacking guacamole.

INGREDIENTS-

– 1 Fully Ripe Avocado
– ½ Cup Finely Chopped Tomato
– 4-5 Cherry Tomatoes (optional)
– ¼ Finely Chopped Onion
– A Handful of Coriander Leaves
– A Pinch of Asafoetida
– ½ Juiced Lemon
– 2 Tbsp Peanuts
– Salt as per Taste
– 1Tbsp **#FEEL GOOD**

METHOD-

Combine all the ingredients in a mixer and make a smooth paste.

Store in a stainless-steel container and refrigerate. This dip can be used for 3-4 days.

8. Tahini

The raw tahini is a bit bitter in taste, so this goes well with sweet vegetables and is also a very good addition to other dips because of the oily texture achieved while grinding the sesame seeds.

INGREDIENTS-

– 1 Cup White Sesame Seeds (Soaked 8-10hours)
– 2 Small Sliced Fresh Green Chilies
– 3-4 Garlic Cloves
– ½ Tbsp Cayenne Pepper Powder
– 2 Tsp Coconut Oil
– 1 Tbsp Lemon Juice
– 2 Macadamia Nuts (optional)
– Salt as per Taste
– 1Tbsp **#SELF APPRECIATION**

METHOD-

Combine all the above ingredients in a blender and make a fine creamy paste.

Store in a glass container for 10 days.

9. Guava Tangy Grape Dip

This tangy mint dip is the juiciness of grapes and freshness of mint leaves which you can relish with any vegetable salad.

INGREDIENTS-

– 1 Cup Fresh Mint Leaves
– 1 Small Piece of Guava
– 10 to 12 Grapes
– Salt as per Taste
– 1 Tbsp #FEEL FRESH

METHOD-

Combine all the ingredients in a mixer and make a smooth paste.

Store in a stainless-steel container and refrigerate. This dip can be used for 3-4 days.

10. Sushi Dressing

This dressing is a balance between the creaminess of the mayo and sharpness of the tart. This will go perfectly well with raw sushi and other salads too.

INGREDIENTS-

– 1 Cup Young Thai Coconut Flesh
– 3 Tbsp Raw Cashews (soaked overnight in water, rinsed and drained well)
– ½ Tbsp Freshly Grated Ginger
– 1 Small Chili
– 1 Garlic Clove
– 1 Tbsp Oregano
– ¼ Tsp Cayenne Pepper
– 1 Tbsp Lime Juice
– ¼ Tbsp Pepper
– A Pinch of Salt
– 1Tbsp #DREAMSCOMETRUE

METHOD-

Combine all ingredients and blend until it forms a smooth, runny and creamy sushi dressing.

Store in a glass jar and refrigerate.

Raw Smoothie Formula

Base Fruit + Liquid- Water/Plant Based Milk
+ Sweetener if needed + Condiment to FLAVOUR

*For food mixing please refer to food combination chapter (Pg No. 13)

1. Coco Chikoo Blend

INGREDIENTS-

To blend -
- 4 Chikoo/Sapodilla
- 1 Glass Coconut Milk
- 1 Tbsp Peanut Butter
- 1 Tbsp Organic Cacao Powder
- 2 Pinch Ground Cardamom
- 6 Ice Cubes (You can use normal water too)
- 1 Tbsp #GOODVibes

To garnish-
- Peanut Butter, Muesli, Cacao nibs

METHOD-

Put all the above ingredients to blend in a mixer or blender to make a smoothie and then top it with the ingredients to garnish. It is a very soothing smoothie for any time of the day. Chikoo contains antioxidants that reduces wrinkle, softens the hair and makes the skin glow.

2. Banana Apple Smash

INGREDIENTS-

To blend -
- 2 Fresh Bananas
- 1 Cup or 20 Leaves Baby Spinach
- ½ Apple
- 1 Fig Ring
- 1 Walnut
- 1 Cup Coconut Milk
- 1 Cup Fresh Water
- 2 Pinch Ground Cardamom
- 1 Tbsp Coconut Palm Sugar/ Jaggery
- 1 Tbsp #PASSION

To garnish-
- Thinly sliced Apple, 10 Soaked Black raisin,4 Crushed Pecan Nuts/ Walnut

METHOD-

Put all the above ingredients to blend in a mixer or blender to make a smoothie and then top it with the ingredients to garnish. Bananas are a good source of carbohydrates, good to consume after a high-intensity workout to restore the glycogen stores that were lost during the workout.

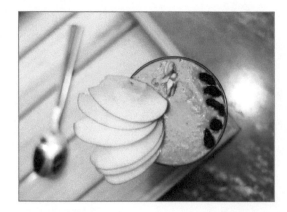

3. Avocado Fig Wonder

INGREDIENTS-

To blend -
– ½ Avocado
– 2 Figs (Fresh/Soaked)
– 1 Fully Ripe Banana or Sweet Seasonal Fruit
– 1 Cup Fresh Water
– 1 Tbsp Organic Jaggery Powder
– 1 Tbsp #TRUTH

To garnish-
– Nutmeg Powder, Muesli, Macadamia Nuts, Sliced Banana, Fresh Coconut Slices.
– 1 Tbsp #NOURISHMENT

METHOD-

Put all the above ingredients to blend in a mixer or blender to make a smoothie and then top them with the ingredients to garnish. It is a very nourishing smoothie for kids and pregnant women.

4. Pineapple Almond Milk

INGREDIENTS-

To blend -
– 3 Slices of Pineapple
– 1 Cup Almond Milk
– 4 Soaked Dates
– 1 Cup Water
– ½ Tbsp Vanilla Pod Powder
– 1 Cup #GRATITUDE

To garnish-
– Pineapple Slices, Almonds

METHOD-

Put all the above ingredients to blend in a mixer or blender to make a smoothie and then top it with the ingredients to garnish. It is a very tasty and tangy smoothie which is superb for thyroid health.

5. Nutella Smoothie

INGREDIENTS-

To blend -
- 1 Tbsp Cacao/Maca Powder
- ½ Fully Ripe Pear (optional)
- 3 Tsp Coconut Oil
- 1 Small Piece Cacao Butter
- 3-4 Macadamia Nut /Cashew
- ¼ Tbsp Cinnamon
- 3 Tbsp Organic jaggery Powder
- Ice Cubes (if needed)
- 1 Cup #ADVENTURE

To garnish-
- Cacao Nibs, Macadamia Nut, Edible Flowers

METHOD-

Put all the above ingredients to blend in a mixer or blender to make a creamy icy smoothie and top it with the ingredients to garnish. It is a very yummy mood enhancer shake for any time of the day.

6. Strawberry Blush

INGREDIENTS-

- 2 Cups of Frozen or Fresh Strawberries
- 1 Soaked Dates or 1Tbsp Maple Syrup
- 1 Cup Coconut Milk
- ½ Cup Water
- 2 Tbsp Jaggery Powder/ Coconut Palm Sugar/ Dates Pulp
- 1 Tbsp Avocado
- ¼ Tbsp Vanilla Pod Powder
- 1 Cup #TRANSFORMATION

METHOD-

Put all the ingredients into a blender and blend until well combined, creamy, icy and smooth. Berries are superb for immunity and are packed with vitamins, fiber, and high levels of antioxidants.

HEAL AND BEYOND

38

7. Pink Rose Smoothie

INGREDIENTS-

To blend -
– ½ Cup Pink Rose Petals Dried
– 2 Pinch Sea Salt
– 1 Tbsp Rose Water
– ½ Cup Almond Milk
– 3 or 4 Pitted Dates
– ½ Cup Coconut Meat
– ¼ Tbsp Javitri Powder
– 3 Paan Leaves
– 1 Cup **#RELAXATION**

To garnish-
– Fresh Rose Petals & Almonds

METHOD-

Put all the above ingredients to blend in a mixer or blender to make a smoothie and then top it with the ingredients to garnish. It is a very refreshing and revitalising drink especially for summers.

8. OMG Berry Rush

INGREDIENTS-

To blend -
– 5-6 Soaked almonds
– 1/3 Cup of Strawberries/Goji Berries/ Blueberries
– 1 Whole Vanilla Pod or 2 Pinch Vanilla Pod Powder
– 2 Dates (optional)
– 3 Oranges, Juiced
– A Tray of Ice (more if you like it really icy)
– 1 Cup **#INTENTION**

METHOD-

Put all the above ingredients to blend in a mixer or blender to make a smoothie and then top it with the ingredients to garnish.

9. Coconut Meat Smoothie

INGREDIENTS-

To blend -
– 1 Cup Coconut Meat
– 1 Glass Coconut Water
– 2 Walnuts Soaked
– 4-5 Kesar Threads
– 2 Soaked Figs
– A Pinch of Salt
– 1 Tbsp **#GRACE**

METHOD-

Put all the above ingredients to blend in a mixer or blender to make a creamy smoothie. Coconut meat is known to help lose weight and ease digestion.

10. Yum Mango Lassi

INGREDIENTS-

To blend -
– 1 Medium Ripe Mango Peeled and Diced
– 2 Tbsp Pistachio
– 3 Dates
– 2 Tbsp Jaggery Powder
– Grated Lemon Zest
– 1 Cup Water or Ice Cubes
– 1 Cup **#LOVE**

To garnish-
– Grounded Nutmeg
– Cardamom to Garnish
– Mango Cubes

METHOD-

Put all the above ingredients to blend in a mixer or blender to make a creamy icy smoothie and then top it with the ingredients to garnish. Mango aids immunity, iron absorption, growth and repair for the body.

Live Juices

41

1. Cabala

INGREDIENTS-

- 5-6 Carrots
- 1 Diced Small Whole Lemon with the Peel
- 1 Red Apple
- 1 Green Apple
- 1 Yellow Apple (optional)
- 1 Small Beetroot with Leaves
- 1 Cup #HAPPINESS

METHOD-

You can use a cold pressed juicer or a centrifugal juicer to juice the ingredients. This juice is amazing for skin, blood circulation and eyes. I also call it the glow juice.

If you do not have all three varieties of apple, use the red apples instead.

2. Sunshine

INGREDIENTS-

- 2 Cups Diced Pineapple
- 3 Peeled Oranges
- 1 Small Fresh Turmeric Root
- 1 Cup #POSITIVITY

METHOD-

You can use a cold pressed juicer or a centrifugal juicer to juice the ingredients. Sunshine juice is now ready to devour. This juice is amazing for the Endocrine system & the bromelain in pineapple is a superb cleanser for the body.

HEAL AND BEYOND

3. Bone Health Juice

INGREDIENTS-

– 1 Cup Diced Apples
– 1 Cup Pomegranate
– 1 Stalks Celery
– 1 Cup Fresh Mint Leaves
– 1 Tsp Lemon Juice
– 1 Cup #STRENGTH

METHOD-

Juice the Apples, Pomegranate, Mint leaves, and Celery in a cold pressed juicer.

Mix all the other ingredients in a jar, add squeezed lemon juice.

If you do not have access to fresh organic celery, you can use coriander or banana plantains. Do not juice the plantain in the juicer, instead use a mixer.

Consume the juice immediately once prepared.

4. Green Bliss

INGREDIENTS-

– 200 gms Green Leafy Vegetables (Spinach, Coriander and Mint leaves)
– 1 Small Bottle Gourd
– 1 Apple/Guava/Pear
– 1 Lemon with Peel
– 1 Inch of Ginger
– 1 Cup #POWER

METHOD-

Use a cold press juicer or use a mixer to grind everything and then sieve it. This is literally a green chlorophyll rich juice glass. It is amazing for cleaning the blood and clearing the skin.

5. Pink Blush

INGREDIENTS-

- 1 Beetroot with Leaves
- 1 Glass Water
- 1 Small Lemon
- 1 Tsp Dry Mint Leaves
- A Pinch of Jeera Powder
- A Pinch of Pink Salt, Black Salt
- 1 Pinch Asafoetida
- 1 Cup #CALMNESS

METHOD-

Use a cold press juicer or use a mixer to grind everything and then sieve it.

Now add water to the concentrated beetroot juice, mix all the other ingredients to get a tangy tasty pink blush.

Beetroot is a great source of folate (vitamin B9), manganese, potassium, iron.

HEAL AND BEYOND

6. Cucumber Flush

INGREDIENTS-

- 1 Big Diced Cucumber
- 1 Lemon with Peel
- 3 Inches of Sweet Aloe Vera Leaf
- 1 Cup #FRESHNESS

METHOD-

Step 1: Juice the cucumbers and lemon in a cold pressed juicer or use a mixer to churn them and then sieve it to get the juice.
Step 2: Take out the pulp from the Aloe vera leaf, add 30ml of water and blend it to make a fine solution.
Step 3: Once blended, sieve the mixture to get a diluted aloe vera juice.
Step 4: Add the aloe vera mixture to the already prepared cucumber lemon juice. Enjoy the cucumber flush.

This combination is amazing for skin & hair. It completely hydrates the body and removes all the toxins out and also acts as a healing juice for thyroid imbalance.

7. Ashgourd or Safed Petha Juice

INGREDIENTS-

– 2 Slices of Ash Gourd [Safed Petha]
– ½ Glass Normal Water or Coconut Water
– 1 Cup #CLARITY

METHOD-

Use a cold pressed juicer to juice the ash gourd or grind the ash gourd in a mixer and strain it. Ashgourd has the ability to literally suck the toxins out of your body. It has an intrinsic expectorant quality, which implies that it can readily loosen any excess phlegm.

8. Citrus Love

INGREDIENTS-

– 2 Oranges
– 3 Sweet Limes
– 10 Basil Leaves
– 1 Cup #EXCITEMENT

METHOD-

Peel the oranges and sweet lime and use a cold pressed juicer to juice the oranges, sweet lime and basil leaves together. The freshness of basil fully enhances the taste and flavour of this combination.

Get your dose of natural Vitamin C when seasonally available.

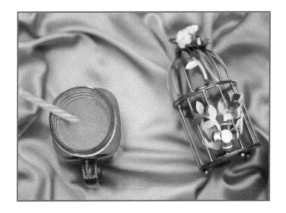

45

9. Sangria

INGREDIENTS-

- 3 Cup Grapes
- 1 Apple
- 1 Kiwi
- 1 Lemon
- ½ Cup Strawberry
- 1 Cup #KINDNESS

METHOD-

Step 1: Juice the grapes, apple, and kiwi in a slow cold pressed juicer.
Step 2: Blend the strawberry in a mixer with the freshly squeezed juice.

Sangria is a very tasty and fruity combination loaded with heaps of natural goodness.

10. Morning Shots

INGREDIENTS-

A) Barley Grass 10 to 12 Leaves Freshly Grown
B) 2 Grated Amla (Indian Gooseberry)
C) 1/2 Inch Raw Grated Turmeric, 1 Orange
D) Handful Coriander, Mint, Tulsi , Lemon

METHOD-

Step for A: Take 30ml water in the mixer and add the barley grass, blend it completely and sieve the solution, your barley grass shot is ready!
Step for B: Grate the amla using a grater, take a thin muslin cloth and squeeze the juice. Your Amla shot is ready!
Step for C: You can use a cold pressed juicer to simply juice the turmeric root and orange.
Step for D: All the green ingredients can be either juiced in a cold pressed juicer or you can take 30ml water in the mixer and blend the ingredients and later sieve it.

Appreciate your mornings by giving the body a light, seasonal and powerful herbal shot.

Raw Desserts

1. High Energy Balls

Instead of buying a protein bar from the shops — because that is what we seem to do — these balls are incredibly easy to make. They bring families together because the kids love rolling them. Pop them in the fridge, in a container and have them on tap before or after a workout. These balls are a great energy lift for your day

INGREDIENTS-

- 1 Cup Almond Flour
- 1 Cup Shredded Fresh Coconut
- 1 Cup Chopped Dates
- 2 Tbsp Cocoa Powder
- 1 Tbsp Black and White Sesame Seeds
- 1 Tbsp Water
- A Pinch of Salt
- 1 Tbsp #HAPPYDAYS

METHOD-

Combine all ingredients in a food processor and process until well combined and sticky enough to roll into balls. Makes 18–20 balls.

2. Minty Cookies

These mint frozen cookies are a full-flavoured mint sensation that is light and refreshing to the palate. These cookies can be made and left in the freezer to be consumed whenever a sweet and minty delicacy is craved.

INGREDIENTS-

- ½ Cup Cocoa Powder
- 1/3 Cup Cashew Butter (simply blending the cashews without any water)
- 2 Cups Shredded Coconut
- 2 Tbsp of Peppermint Leaf Powder
- ½ Cup Maple Syrup (or Sweetener of your choice)
- 2 Tbsp Jaggery Powder
- A Pinch of Salt
- 1 Cup #JUST BREATHE

METHOD-

Combine all ingredients in a food processor and process until well combined (until sticky). Form into round balls and push down into a cookie shape. Place onto a tray, freeze for 30 minutes, and store in a container.

3. Carrot Beetroot Mud Cake

This cake is genius. The beetroot and the coconut create such sweet flavours that marry up with the cocoa. The icing alone is rich, thick, and decadent, and you would never realise that it does not contain dairy. Cut into squares and pop in the freezer, you have a high plant-based dessert on tap. I learnt this from an amazing chef when I was in Bali.

INGREDIENTS-

For Base-
– 1 Medium Sized Grated Beetroot
– 1 Large, Grated Carrot
– 2 Cups Shredded Coconut
– 2 Tbsp Psyllium Husk (Isabghol)
– 15 Dried Dates, 3-4tsp Liquid Jaggery or Molasses
– 1 Cup Cocoa Powder
– 100gm Soaked Almonds (soaked overnight in 2 cups of water, rinsed well and drained)
– ¼ Cup Chia Seeds, A Pinch of Salt
– 1 Tbsp #JOY

For Icing-
– ½ Cup Cocoa Powder
– 1 Cup Soaked Cashews (soaked overnight in 2 cups of water and drained well)
– ¼ Cup chia seeds
– 2/3 Cup Maple Syrup or Natural Sweetener
– ½ Cup Water
– ½ Cup Coconut Oil
– 2 Tsp of Cocoa Butter (optional)

METHOD-

Base Method - Combine all base ingredients in a food processor and process until you get a well combined dough. Transfer into a round cake tin, press the dough down to get an even layer. Set aside in the fridge while you make the icing.

Icing Method - Combine the first five icing ingredients in a blender and blend until creamy and smooth. Once creamy and smooth, turn the blender down to medium speed and pour in the melted cocoa butter/coconut oil. Blend for 5 seconds, pour onto the cake, and refrigerate the cake for minimum 6 hours to set and firm up for the icing to set and the cake to firm up.

49

4. Date Éclair

A perfect reward to kids, get rid of processed packaged chocolates & make a few for your family at home. These Eclairs are simply ultimate.

INGREDIENTS-

For Peanut Butter:
– 1 Cup Peanut
– 1/3 Cup Coconut Sugar
– A Pinch of Salt

For Date Éclair Coating:
– 5 Big Sized Medjool Dates
– 1 Cup Coconut Sugar
– 20ml Coconut Oil
– 4 Tbsp Jaggery Powder
– 4 Tbsp Organic Cacao Powder
– 1 Tbsp Maca Powder (optional)
– Salt
– ¼ Cup Water
– 1 Tbsp **#STRESS FREE**

METHOD-

For the Peanut Butter:
- Grind the 1 cup peanuts, 1/3 cup coconut sugar and a pinch of salt in a high-speed blender until it forms a buttery texture.
- Slit the Date open, remove the seed and enormously fill the date with peanut butter.

For the Chocolate Coating:
Combine all the ingredients of Date Éclair coating in a high-speed blender to form a thick runny chocolate paste.

For the Date Éclair:
Now your peanut butter filled dates are ready to be coated with homemade chocolate. Coat the Date Éclair with chocolate and garnish with peanut crunch and refrigerate for 5-6 hours until the chocolate completely hugs the date. Eat them and enjoy.

5. Coconut Milk Vanilla Custard

This creamy custard is so satisfying and tasty that you will not even realize that it has no dairy & no refined sugar in it. Coconut milk contains antioxidants, helps in electrolyte balance and strengthens the immune system.

INGREDIENTS-

- 1 Glass Freshly Squeezed Coconut Milk
- ½ Cup Finely Chopped Apple
- ½ Cup Finely Chopped Banana
- ½ Cup Finely Chopped Chikoo/Sapodilla
- ½ Cup Pomegranate
- 2 Tbsp Coconut Palm Sugar or Jaggery Powder
- 5-6 Saffron Threads
- 2 Tbsp Crushed Pistachio
- A Pinch of Vanilla Pod Powder
- 1Tbsp #RELAXATION

Coconut milk is a white, milky substance extracted from the flesh of mature fresh brown coconuts. It is a versatile ingredient and an excellent animal milk alternative. Consumption of coconut milk in moderation gives health benefits. Vanilla bean powder used in the custard gives a strong aromatic, warm and floral flavour. It is a gentle but distinct flavour that complements perfectly with coconut milk.

METHOD-

Make fresh coconut milk using 3 glasses of water and 1 full coconut in a mixer and then sieve the mixture to extract fresh milk. Combine all the above ingredients in the coconut milk and refrigerate the custard. You can eat this for up to the next 3-4 days.

Infused Water

1. Strawberry Infused Water

Strawberry is nutrient rich and packed with antioxidants. Basil contains magnesium, which helps to improve blood flow by allowing muscles and blood vessels to relax. When this combination is infused in water you will be able to meet your daily hydration goals easily. Adding sliced fruits and torn herbs are a simple way to boost the flavour.

INGREDIENTS-

- 3 Glass Filtered Water
- 5-6 Pieces of Strawberry
- 10 Fresh Leaves of Basil
- 1 Whole Lemon, Sliced

METHOD-

Step 1: Fill the jar with 3 glass of filtered water and add 5-6 pieces of strawberries, 10 leaves of basil and sliced lemon.
Step 2: Stir water with strawberries, lemon and basil together in a big jar.
Step 3: Allow the mixture to sleep in the refrigerator or a cool dark place for 4-8 hours.
For best flavour and health benefits, consume within 24-48 hours.

2. Orange Infused Water

Orange ginger infused water not only boosts your metabolism, but also helps you fight a cold and stay healthy. Ginger provides anti-inflammatory benefits which aids in joint pain and is known for helping with digestion and nausea.

INGREDIENTS-

- 3 Glass Filtered Water.
- 1 Navel Orange Cut into thin Rings.
- ½ inch Fresh Ginger, Peeled and Thinly Sliced.
(you can vary the quantity as per your need)

NOTE: DO NOT SQUEEZE THE CITRUS, YOU WOULD ADD TOO MUCH OF THEIR FLAVOUR TO THE WATER.

METHOD-

Step 1: Wash the orange fruit and ginger before adding them to the water.
Step 2: Fill the jar with 3 glass of filtered water, add sliced orange and thinly sliced ginger.
Step 3: Refrigerate overnight, then drink within 24 hours.

After 24 hours, the aromatics might release too much flavour and you may not like it.

53

3. Pineapple Infused Water

This concoction is an excellent super food for thyroid health; it helps in digestion because it is full of digestive- boosting enzymes along with this, it also helps in liver cleansing.
It is a good source of potassium, calcium, sodium & is loaded with antioxidants.

INGREDIENTS-

– 3 Glass Filtered Water
– 2-3 Thin Slices of Pineapple
– 2-inch Fresh Coconut
– 1 Whole Lemon, Sliced.

METHOD-

Step 1: Fill the jar with 3 glasses of filtered water, add thin slices of pineapple, coconut, and lemon.
Step 2: Stir and place in the fridge for couple of hours.

For best flavour and health benefits, consume within 24-48 hours.

4. Apple Infused Water

Apple contains pectin and helps remove heavy metals from your body while cinnamon helps to stabilize blood sugar. This water works wonder to flush toxins out of the body.

INGREDIENTS-

– 2 Glasses of Filtered Water
– 1 Cinnamon Stick
– 1 Apple Thinly Sliced
– 1 Star Anise (Chakraphool)

METHOD-

Step 1: Cut the apple into large chunks. Be sure you leave the skin on.
Step 2: Fill the mason jar with filtered water, add thin slices of apple, the stick of cinnamon and star anise to the jar.
Step 3: Let sit overnight in the refrigerator and keep it next to your worktable.

This will help you stay hydrated and also add extra dose of vitamins to your water.

5. Cucumber Infused Water

Rose petals help in relieving stress and uplifting your mood, while cucumber is one of the most readily available ingredients in the market which keeps you hydrated. This infused water ensures weight loss, better digestion and eases nausea.

INGREDIENTS-

- 2 Glass Filtered Water
- 1 Cucumber Thinly Sliced.
- Handful of Rose Petals.
- 5-6 Grapes

METHOD-

Step 1: Fill the jar with 2 glass of filtered water, take a handful of rose petals, thinly sliced cucumber and grapes cut in halves.

Step 2: Mix all the ingredients and let it stay for 4-5 hours. Drink in a duration of 24 hours before the concoction becomes too loud.

Conclusion

What is the right thing to do? For your body, for nature, for health and for our future generations. There is a very deep and profound connection between the way we think, feel, eat and behave. I would just suggest you to take that small step and just begin at your own space & pace. I hope you will try and inculcate fresh foods in your everyday plate. Health, immunity and well being is not achieved overnight; it is gained by practicing active and correct lifestyle every single day. Out of 30 days in a month, make sure that you are getting the raw dose at least 25 days. Don't lose hope, don't lose confidence, don't lose consistency. Everything is possible.

Lots of Love,

Nidhi Jagetia

Raw Food Pantry Basics

i. Pantry Items

Sweeteners

Few natural sweeteners such as jaggery powder, coconut palm sugar, molasses, maple syrup and medjool dates are used throughout the recipes, and sometimes used in pairs. All these natural sweeteners are wonderful in flavour. You can easily get all of them and always focus more on the one closest to nature, with low human interference and local availability.

Salt

Himalayan crystal salt (both pink and black) or local rock salt have amazing flavour and beneficial health properties. Salts have an unbelievable amount of trace-essential minerals. The salt should be an Aluminium free salt. Eating too much salt is not healthy, so only add salts to enhance the taste of the dish, keeping it fresh and tasty.

Coconut oil

There are many types of coconut oil available in the market. I prefer using cold pressed oil. The coconuts come from one plantation, and the oil is produced at a shop in front of my eyes — unrefined and unscented and full of goodness. You can find a similar setup as its cheaper and trustful. Don't go overboard with the oil, it is for occasional delicacies.

Herbs & Spices

Here is a list to get you started- himalayan salt (pink), celtic sea salt, black peppercorns, cumin seeds, caraway seeds, coriander seeds, mustard seeds, curry powder (ground), nutmeg, cinnamon, cardamom, star anise, paprika, cayenne pepper, vanilla beans or a good quality vanilla pod powder.

I prefer to buy all the spices in their whole form (even salt and pepper). They are easy to grind and their fresh aroma is prominent in the recipes. These spices are an important part of whole-food dishes, as these are the building blocks of flavour. Grinding the spices ourselves is as easy as putting them into your blender and pushing "blend" till you get a ground mix.

Cacao

There is so much info on free web about the benefits of cacao, so I will keep this simple. Not all cacao is roasted, but it is fermented to reduce the bitterness. It is fully flavoured and full of natural goodness. The beans on the inside of the pod are fermented and used in confections, potions, and brews. Cacao comes in the form of whole beans, nibs, powder and cacao butter. It is available in raw form too so I would recommend getting an organic, raw cacao powder and satiate your taste buds with the chocolaty flavour.

56

Nuts & Seeds
Here is a list- almonds, cashews, brazil nuts, macadamia, pistachio, walnuts, coconut dry (unbleached) shredded, coconut fresh, sunflower seeds, sesame seeds (black and white), chia seeds (white and black).

Store all the nuts in a deep freezer and the seeds in a fridge, both sealed well.

I have added the soaking process when using nuts for two reasons: Firstly, to bring them to life by adding water and allowing the nut to begin to grow. Secondly, the strong flavour is mostly gone after a good soaking. I don't particularly want to taste nut flavour throughout, so soaking is a great way to cut that extra flavour out when making some of the dressings and smoothies.

ii. Equipments

Blender
This is one of the major tools when it comes to raw eating. I use Vitamix and sometimes the small pot (chutney pot) of regular mixer which also gives a smooth paste. Blender is a one-stop shop for combining and making some of the best raw dishes.

Knife
Buy a good knife! I own a Victorinox knife and a peeler & I absolutely love it. You can also use any other knife which is well sharpened.

Juicing & Juicer
Juicing is extracting the organic water from fruits and vegetables, which concentrates the vitamins and minerals by removing the pulp and fiber. Juicing is a great way to stay hydrated and enjoy a wide range of nutrition. It is extremely good for cleansing and healing the body.

A slow pressed juicer is better than a normal juicer. Why?

A slow pressed juicer yields a higher amount of juice with little to no oxidation, and a higher mineral content along with beneficial essential oils from the produce.

Yes, the price is higher, but we cannot really put a value on optimal health.

Micro plane
It is a kind of a kitchen grater used for the grating of various food items such as nutmeg, ginger, and garlic, and also zesters.

Food Processor
A food processor is an absolute essential in the kitchen.
You can use it for so many jobs- everything from grating to mincing to mixing. It's a super time saving device in the kitchen.

Nidhi Jagetia

Best Out of Waste

Composting and Recycling

Composting and Recycling in today's world are the ideal ways to reduce our carbon footprints on the planet. Earth's resources are exhaustible and pollution is damaging, to mitigate a part of this problem we can convert the edible waste into highly valuable nutrients-rich compost.

Composting is beautiful, as it both eliminates all the organic waste in a conscious way and fertilizes the soil for future growth. Vermicompost improves growth, quality and yield of different crops. It contributes to recycling of nitrogen and augments soil physicochemical as well as biological properties. By producing less waste, we help make the future brighter.

When the kitchen scraps are thrown away in a plastic bag and sent to landfill, it releases methane, a greenhouse gas which is more potent than carbon dioxide! And the benefits of that organic waste are lost forever. Composting can help us cut down on waste and turn the kitchen scraps back into a usable resource.

CPSIA information can be obtained
at www.ICGtesting.com
Printed in the USA
BVHW022243210721
612426BV00002B/22